WITH NO BRIDLE
FOR THE BREEZE

Elizabeth Spencer Spragins

WITH NO BRIDLE FOR THE BREEZE

Ungrounded Verse

poems by

Elizabeth Spencer Spragins

Shanti Arts Publishing

Brunswick, Maine

WITH NO BRIDLE FOR THE BREEZE
Ungrounded Verse

Published by Shanti Arts Publishing
Designed by Shanti Arts Designs

Shanti Arts LLC
193 Hillside Road
Brunswick, Maine 04011
shantiarts.com

Cover photograph: Mantonature /
1002681438 / istockphoto.com

Printed in the United States of America

ISBN: 978-1-947067-90-5 (softcover)

Library of Congress Control Number: 2019943450

For Mike,
who has walked beside me
on so many journeys

CONTENTS

FEATHERS

MIRRORRED WINGS

DREAMS

Acknowledgements

I am deeply grateful to the following journals and anthologies, in which some of these poems first appeared:

Adelaide
Ariel Chart
Atlas Poetica 26
Atlas Poetica 30
Atlas Poetica: Dream Alchemy
Blueline
Borrowed Solace
Flash & Cinder
Folded Word
Founder's Favorites
Halcyon Days
Page & Spine
Peacock Journal
Poetry Quarterly
*Wild Voices, Vol. 2: An Anthology of Short
      Poetry & Art by Women*
Words for the Wild

FEATHERS

REFLECTIONS

cerulean blue
painted on the backs of birds —
a pale patch of sky
nestles deep in cotton quilts
scented with an April rain

~ Deep Creek Lake State Park,
Swanton, Maryland

Morning Sparks

when the sun kindles
waters soft and still with sleep
a goldfinch blazes
through the crack where dark meets dawn
on wings that beat like bellows

~ Potomac River, Fairview Beach, Virginia

TORRENTS

when this river roars
the red oak rocks her cradle —
a nest that slumbers
high above the turbulence
holds certainty of swallows

~ Rappahannock River,
Fredericksburg, Virginia

CARESS

tree swallows twitter
outside my bedroom window
just before daybreak
a breeze fondles lace curtains
and I turn toward unseen touch

~ Charleston, South Carolina

Kindling

cardinals nesting
on the chapel window ledge —
a shard of stained glass
hidden in the brittle grass
catches fire at break of day

~ Toano, Virginia

RAIN DROPS

two great-tailed grackles
strut through puddles on my lawn —
folded umbrellas
stitched with iridescent beads
shimmer in the slanted light

~ Fredericksburg, Virginia

CHAMBER MUSIC

a maidenhair fern
rises from her mossy bed
to flutes of thrushes
breezes tune the fiddleheads
and coax blues from violas

> ~ Meadowlark Botanical Gardens,
> Vienna, Virginia

Holding Hands

tulip petals droop
beneath the weight of water
cupped in open palms
feathered dandelion dust
drifts away on breath of dreams

~ Wiscasset, Maine

Nests

three beaks open wide
at the fluttering of wings —
a plain wooden bowl
veined with memories of drought
cradles dusty walnut shells

~ Omaha, Nebraska

NECTAR

a split-rail fence sags
beneath honeysuckle vines
hummingbirds gather
the thick perfume of summer
sweetness lingers on my tongue

~ Fredericksburg, Virginia

ACROBATICS

a tree swallow swings
through the sultry afternoon —
unhanded trapeze
slowly arcs through open air
a breath beyond the unfledged

~ Fredericksburg, Virginia

WALTZING WITH THE WIND

wings of an eagle
waltz across a cloudless sky —
soft summer music
glides across the forest floor
awhirl with lady slippers

> ~ Meadowview Biological Research Station,
> Woodford, Virginia

PALETTES

gradients of green
blend beneath the sapphire sky
within this woodland
a yellow-throated warbler
colors silence with her song

~ Pisgah National Forest,
North Carolina

CLARITY

cotton clouds adrift
on this liquid looking glass
beneath the mountain
a stately great blue heron
slowly walks across the sky

~ Ticonderoga, New York

Night Fog

an autumn sun sinks
into quilted quietness —
lullabies of loons
ferry me to forest realms
and drift on dreams till daylight

~ Damariscotta, Maine

FLAMES

two red-shouldered hawks
spiral over crimson clouds —
torches without fire
kindle leaves of linden trees
in defiance of the dark

~ Damariscotta, Maine

Beyond Sight

quiet curtains fall
on silhouettes of cedars
rooted in the mist
sailboats drowse to songs of owls
and laments of buoy bells

> ~ Deep Creek Lake State Park,
> Swanton, Maryland

Night Music

a bent longleaf pine
holds the sun in calloused hands
behind curtained clouds
winds that walk the woodlands hum
faded notes of mockingbirds

~ Asheville, North Carolina

DESCANT

evensong of owls
echoes through the emptiness
in hidden hollows
footfalls of coyote clans
follow music of old moons

~ Flagstaff, Arizona

THE COLOR WHEEL

a rainbow arrows
over clouds weighted with gray
mirrored in the loch
a golden eagle spirals
toward promises of sunlight

~ Loch Lomond, Scotland

Owls

soundless silhouettes
coast on currents of the sky
between dusk and dark
a harvest moon balances
on fingertips of birches

~ Caledon State Park,
King George, Virginia

STEALTH

twin moons rise slowly
in the golden eyes of owls
silently waiting
I will my breath to stillness
but cannot hold my heartbeat

~ Caledon State Park,
King George, Virginia

Coveted

a set of fox tracks
leads to blackberry brambles
dusted with new snow
agitated chickadees
defend the barren branches

~ Willow Spring, North Carolina

EMBERS

a red dawn blazes
on an unexpected snow —
two cardinals perch
on a frosted wrought-iron fence
that sparks in slanted sunlight

~ Charleston, South Carolina

UNTHAWED

the junco perches
on a frosted linden limb
where gray lies buried
sunlight skates on frozen pools
and cuts the cold with diamonds

~ Appomattox Court House, Virginia

TIES

firs feathered with frost
lift their limbs into the wind
beneath an eagle
thin ribbons of a river
tether earth to cloudy skies

~ Middlebury, Vermont

WHEN LIGHT FADES

pine shadows lengthen
as a blue heron hunches
over gray waters
distorted by thunder clouds
I stand without reflection

~ Woodbridge, Virginia

WHITE FIRE

a sleepy sunrise
nestles deep in downy quilts —
flurries of feathers
dust a winterberry branch
draped with beads that burn the snow

~ Williamsburg, Virginia

MIRRORED WINGS

Bejeweled

daybreak burns the dew
from leaves of mountain laurel —
untamed emeralds
that take wing with damselflies
hover lightly in the heart

> ~ Meadowlark Botanical Gardens,
> Vienna, Virginia

TOURNAMENT

honeybees gather
in a field of wildflowers
bold hummingbirds joust
for golden cups of nectar
and honeysuckle trumpets

~ Appomattox Court House, Virginia

Summer Lightning

lanterns of fireflies
wink to slow summer rhythms —
garden fairy lights
kindle memories of jars
filled with sparks of childhood dreams

~ Willow Spring, North Carolina

FORGING FAIRY STONES

the stones remember
heartbeats of a Beltane blaze
when fireflies gather
diamond dust of fallen stars
faeries dance till crystals cross

~ Fairy Stone State Park, Stuart, Virginia

THE LAST LIGHT

a swallowtail dips
into nectar of the dusk
as peonies nod
in the cradle of a breeze
daydreams drift on folded wings

> ~ Lewis Ginter Botanical Garden,
> Richmond, Virginia

EVENSONG

when the heavens flame
a great blue heron rises
from depths of stillness
the plainsong of cicadas
calls mourning doves to compline

~ Rappahannock River,
Fredericksburg, Virginia

Unreined

when the daylight leans
dragonflies unfetter fire —
iridescent wings
balance on a summer sigh
with no bridle for the breeze

> ~ Lewis Ginter Botanical Garden,
> Richmond, Virginia

Blueberries

a painted lady
sips the sun from blazing stars
heavy with honey
pearls of powdered blue fall free
as bracelets break from branches

~ Dunellen, New Jersey

MOONLIGHT

wings of Luna moths
lift their mirrored pairs of eyes —
the moon walks lightly
on slippers trimmed with silver
through a field of faded stars

~ Lewis Ginter Botanical Garden,
Richmond, Virginia

Repose

wicker rockers rest
as porches sag toward twilight
paddle fans balance
on humid breath of August
that holds up lights of fireflies

~ Savannah, Georgia

REGRETS

a hummingbird moth
hovers over wilted phlox
frosted with diamonds
a tall glass of lemonade —
untasted summer sweetness

~ Richmond, Virginia

ALIGHT

lotus leaves gather
diamonds of an autumn rain —
the weight of water
sparks on wings of damselflies
that flame with iridescence

> ~ Kenilworth Park and Aquatic Gardens,
> Washington, DC

Honey Comb

the fragrance of fall
drifts on tides of tangled grass —
a sea of thistles
hums with honey song of bees
that comb the waves of nectar

~ Warrenton, Virginia

DRAGONFLIES

meadows of fireweed
burn beneath an autumn rain —
the flash of diamonds
dances on translucent wings
and lights bejeweled dragons

~ Juneau, Alaska

DREAMS

CLOUDED

a single ripple
stirs the liquid looking glass
where my daydreams drift
a pair of cotton ponies
sails the silence out to sea

> ~ Deep Creek Lake State Park,
> Swanton, Maryland

Racing the Day

when my vessel leaps
and canters through the currents
wind song fills my sails
but in notes of buoy bells
I taste the salt of twilight

~ Annapolis, Maryland

SEAS OF SNOW

the moon sails her skiff
over oceans filled with foam —
waves of combed cotton
glisten on a frozen field
lit by lanterns of the sky

~ Fredericksburg, Virginia

CRESTS

when bliss fills my sail
dolphins frolic in the wake
though I am off course
sunset settles on the bow
and gilded waves guide me home

~ Halifax, Nova Scotia, Canada

LOST

a lone coyote
wanders deserts of the dark
when there is no moon
tarnished stones upon this path
draw my dreams from silvered skies

~ Immigration Detention Center,
Brownsville, Texas

DESERT SNOW

drums sing at twilight
when wind stirs the cottonwoods —
a soft breath of snow
drifts on tides of faded notes
that sail into the silence

~ Santa Fe, New Mexico

Courage

a river of fog
meanders through the boulders —
stepping stones to sea
rise from filaments of dreams
that blanket restless waters

> ~ Rappahannock River,
> Fredericksburg, Virginia

At the Gate of Day

a gray cloak of clouds
swirls and catches in the trees —
dawn wheels her horses
with no thought of bare shoulders
or the darkness left behind

~ Fort Lauderdale, Florida

REFRACTION

cotton horses browse
beyond the rims of rainbows —
I rein my daydreams
as showers blur the edges
of faded watercolors

~ Charlottesville, Virginia

Conquest

as walls etched with moss
encircle castle ruins
reflections waver —
towers mirrored in the loch
fall to winds without a sound

~ Eilean Donan Castle, Dornie, Scotland

LAMENT

a lone piper dreams
upon the hush that hovers
between earth and sky
sacred stone holds castle keep
against the weight of darkness

~ Royal Edinburgh Military Tattoo,
Edinburgh Castle, Scotland

CRIMSON

maples lose their fire
to the feral teeth of wind —
bones of fallen leaves
lie unburied on their backs
and marvel at the sunset

~ Stockbridge, Massachusetts

THE VACANT STUDIO

the spattered sill sags
beneath a box of brushes —
heart of pine splinters
into so many colors
in the darkness of my dreams

> ~ Gari Melchers' Studio at Belmont,
> Fredericksburg, Virginia

Hope

frosted maple leaves
cup cinders of the sunset —
a shower of sparks
thrown to earth by shooting stars
lights the tapers of my dreams

~ Bar Harbor, Maine

FACETS

black velvet cradles
diamonds pressed from darkness —
jewel box of stars
blazes in the silent cold
with dreams adrift on night skies

~ Santa Fe, New Mexico

SHOOTING STAR

fingers of a breeze
sweep the strings that tether stars —
silver serenade
that blazes in the blackness
kindles balefires in my bones

~ Fairbanks, Alaska

CRYSTAL MOMENTUM

the winter river
lingers just before she leaps —
frozen water falls
into silent realms of sleep
that fetter time and sorrow

~ Niagara Falls, New York

Aurora

lamplight cuts the cold
of this lonely land of white
when midnight lingers
magic flames embrace the moon
and dance her dreams with rainbows

~ Fairbanks, Alaska

FIELD OF STARS

the moon meanders
through a meadow thick with stars —
a thousand lanterns
set adrift on lakes of dreams
flicker with forgotten light

~ Fairbanks, Alaska

ANCHORED

a thin slice of moon
tethered just above the trees —
dreams break their bowlines
when cold stars kindle beacons
from embers of the sunset

~ Fredericksburg, Virginia

STILL

the glow of street lamps
cradles falling flakes of snow
on pillows of sleep
murmurs drift into the dark
so soft so cold so quiet

~ Winston-Salem, North Carolina

RESURRECTION

a lean winter wind
gnaws the beauty from each bone —
heartbeats of poppies
pulse within forgotten seeds
hidden in a fallow field

~ Sevilla, Spain

IMMORTAL

cold curtains of fog
veil the face of Denali —
no fear of falling
in dreams my feet are planted
on rungs of stars beyond reach

~ Denali National Park, Alaska

Following the Moon

an unpainted sky
pales to gradients of gray—
the moon veils her face
and glides on silver slippers
into frosted highland hills

~ Glen Coe, Scotland

About the Author

Elizabeth Spencer Spragins is a writer, poet, and editor who taught in North Carolina community colleges for more than a decade. Her tanka and bardic verse in the Celtic style have been published in England, Scotland, Canada, Indonesia, India, Mauritius, and the United States. Recent work has appeared in the *Lyric, Blueline, Atlas Poetica, Page & Spine, Rockvale Review,* and *Halcyon Days.*

— www.authorsden.com/ elizabethspragins

SHANTI ARTS
nature · art · spirit

Please visit us on online

to browse our entire book catalog,

including additional poetry collections and fiction,

books on travel, nature, healing, art,

photography, and more.

shantiarts.com